CYCLONE FENCE

Dale Jensen

Beatitude Press

BERKELEY, CALIFORNIA

For Judy

Copyright © 2007 by Dale Jensen

Book and Cover Designed by Douglas Rees
Cover Photo by the Author

Printed in the United States of America
By Beatitude Press, Berkeley, California

ISBN: 0-9795651-4-6

Some of these poems have appeared in the following anthologies, magazines, and journals: *Ballpeen, Bay Area Poets Seasonal Review, Blindman's Rainbow, Convolvulus, Dirigible, Dream Machinery, Experimental Forest, 5th Wall, Gortday Review, Hogtown Creek Review, Ice River, Juxta, Lost and Found Times, North Coast Literary Review, Oakland (A Literal Reading), Planet Chaos, Poetrymagazine.com, Poets Against the War, Score, Signature Poems, Sivullinen, Southwest Women's Poetry Exchange, tight, Transmog, Ur-Vox,* and *The Walrus.*

Contents

ARCHAEOLOGICAL SITE

call a plumber!
this helicopter
                is digging
             between my temples!
          french fries!
jail!   shoulders!
    knit flags!
politics are my balls!
ape hair   all over the floor!
the middle of dogs doesn't even have
its rubble cleared!
sundays   forbidden
are sold with more sanctity than confetti or scarecrows!
please!
call a plumber!
my walls have been running
and i haven't seen them
for weeks!

AUTOMOBILE LANDSCAPE

he who joys among buses like sharks' teeth
could criticize curses
the woes that go here define the current so swim anyway

and particularly a static land
traffic jams for the centuries
collection of stomachs
a landscape of undetached sleeves
a place that's almost impossible
who would have looked more than i know your vistas

who needs so
upfront:
       1) always be also
       2) heaven and it me
       3) because it's salty and covering their wheels
       4) are not mold wipers

the other source of limousines:
       1) be a mystery to myself
       2) relax and breathe deeply
       3) springing sounds next door
       4) brainfads toward loving broth

someone i love like a motor purr
repeat to me:
       1) has large eyes
       2) hourglass
       3) a boy wants
       4) uncursed and exotic
       5) hubcap

THE BLOOD OF MY RADIO

my radio's blood
              is quaint   evanescent
it seeps into air without touching wood or metal
animals on strange planets worship it
              its grease
              the major tourist attraction
              in thirteen cathedrals

i would kneel to it
but its rhythms
are too irregular
could not sustain
a rodent
even one
wearing an officer's uniform
or a business suit
and holding its breath

so as an entrepreneur
i'm out of business
i can't even sell
its source
since it comes in in waves from someplace else
and my radio's blood
is only a translation
before its own language is conquered
and it disappears

PAINT MAKES THE MAN

room
comes when a man's reason is away
full about these clothes and
to entomb itself
superiority on its part perhaps
paint makes the man   and that's all
it was as if   there on display
group or a whole country's horizons

found a nail that long on the stairway
found rain on the skylight an entire mist
fill em up here surprise that there was
a pill when opened december already
grand lit square of sandstone downtown's river drifting in
contraband bite accompanied by dunes   settlers

PILED MICE

the profundity of no longer being overheard

i place before you piled mice
else's
                refrigerator
as their rumors   carry themselves
boldly
                onto the walls of a museum

you can only visit them there

the symptoms:
                some knives look for success
                even fantasy doesn't work anymore
                cereal section of your supermarket
                and he's not even up for promotion

ENSANE

CELL

imagine any protozoan cell
as a room full of people
nucleus large as an elephant in the middle of the conversations
that people can gawk at
and cilia invisible on the other side of the wall
taking the whole shebang on its way through town

people flow   talk flows
the whole party flows like the totality of plasma
the cowboy stands up there on the butte   pale horse beside him
watches the protozoan row itself giddily through town
down the main street with its lights
cilia happily playing themselves off walls and windows
imagine his laughter

his chaps   the leather of his chaps
his saddle   his horse
all the other various membranes that float through space
all the laughter   all the stillness
all the enclosed laughter

i watched her walk
in the nebulated sunset

my heart is open
as a side of beef

FOR FRANCIS BACON

a house like a museum:
everything fits in
ripped hearts

each particle

claws that are
sinew inside

its breath

this room
its breath
the varying scents of
dogs' voices

my heart is open as a side of beef

you're too young
to get off the stove
and not burn

dogs' voices:

i have kept all my teeth
since childhood
in one pocket
that bulges now
when i walk

that rattles
like breath
when i touch it

WAKING UP ON THE OTHER COAST

dreams   seek   the thin blue lines of blood
the taste of manna is doubt if that's the right city
        cab by   like a jack o lantern
        a reservation that assures that everyone here
        pays off the night
        the grin remaining the next morning
        dawn's dew appears to be time
another cab goes by the wisdom now has congealed into asphalt
        metallic cat's breath
all the humor but really i was born on the wrong coast for this
        manic teeth at the window as the next one goes north
splay-feathered cockroaches eating donuts off the street
the kind they don't make in california
in retroactivity it sounds like complaints through bird teeth
of children playing fire station past extinction time
waiting with their folded sharks' wings
        pastel camouflage
sand now lost to the desert that's built into golden gate park
        masters of ego for that
discovered the next morning under cabbage leaves
restaurants for drowned horses open past midnight
        that's evolution
        and where's that damned cab?
a bus would be a step toward the vindication of dinosaurs
and below all this the subway's running like dreams of blood
corpuscles   embodiment   that's
sweet sleep for eggs

HAD TO BE RITUAL SPACE

when first faced without god figures
and a very pan angry
ignorance
not faced itself
the tapes   concert halls   and sports
make a noise
and produce mural worship

at home we come out of the ends of newspapers

a line being drawn

it is fascinating to obtained through our creative discovery
through a chimpanzee laugh
them after
viewing it seems that we do
very fast
but calling loudly

CULTURE

i have to check your history at four-thirty
all the roman ruins of dehydrated bacteria
all the viral cave paintings of galloping infections
all stretched up and down among the hills and dips
of all the beggars holding previous diagnoses in their broken paws

but now   i want you to take this
volume of medical lore that i'll leave you on your nightstand
look through the pictorial representations
tomorrow i'll give you real ones in a vial
the art from the museum of my soul
the winding and unwinding of the dna of my own civilization
the light that transcends glass
to make its own moon on the wall so to speak
can you sing?   can you sing to this?
your notes will float you away
this cave art newly manufactured
these paintings made of smoke
this memory of their genesis too hot to hold
for longer than the second it takes your mouth to say lifetime

BABEL

In reality there were many towers at Babel, each built by a different manner of being, and in reality few of them fell. The others continued to exist, each invisible and irrelevant to all outside of itself, all eventually forming a network. One tower became the lungs, another the bones, a third the skin, a fourth the heart. Those towers that had fallen formed the brain, babbling at once in many languages, with all of the babblers totally deaf to one another.

AFTER MAX ERNST

now   that   now   that
the the the the
fist is clenched
firecracker explodes
maid scours
wind trims

there on that hill
why haven't they been reported to me?
calendar gun
bottom of the bear fine cilia
forward like that ourselves
like an aphid

ground ground ground ground
fumes fumes fumes fumes
understand how to accommodate yourself
with stalactites as puff pastry

FOUR DICTIONARY POEMS

I   see saw:

      up and down
      contest
      or struggle

      site ends
      of the other goes down

II   security:

      being secure as
      fear or anxiety

      freedom from given

      pledged to make an evidence

      ownership of cures

III   sampling:

      technique pose

      a small part of people

IV   revelation:

      communicating divine
      humans

AUNT GRISELDA SELLS OUT

be sure and leave me
dripping with content
show up again with a normal dust
you the ones who requested this?

i can't see
you described it in a different language
i didn't realize there was no electric stove
in the middle ages and this
the ballot punched the particular person was there

sweepstakes   sweepstakes   sweepstakes   sweepstakes
greenwich village has been full of rich people
for fifty years now

buy broccoli   buy broccoli
buy broccoli   buy broccoli
a mutilation drops her new mug of fresh coffee
aunt griselda sells out

only a sock   only a sock
only a sock   only a sock
items might prove extensively
at home with a pen and a pad of paper

magnifying glass
too much money on the jukebox
is that a bus
or a limousine i just missed?

LAST PURCHASE

civilization won't let you in at the table top
thing in the cold
unaware of
part of you
the dream   cool
of jungle under hands
the part of
when your throat hurts

but often death is less organic but you
a short fast life
these live in   as the clouds move
last purchase
the flood is too cozy
you can't   see them
part of you   the part you   the part of
and can't for the freeze

THE BIG MYSTERY

show up with a normal dust
a leaned forward mousetrap and a bloodstained complaint car

the particular person was there
where warrants are dead

despite the dead
include in the basis:
> it was nine and a nine years
> only a sock
> items might prove extremely call
> since she had agreed in
> for a sick co-worker

curious

items:
> bloody shoe
> bloody handprint
> investigators
> a low monotone

then a week went through the house
> a police magnifying glass
> chemical feet from the ledge

she from florida
was said
> into the metal box
> fingerprints
> in the end

in her nine years of strudel
a mutilation dropped a fresh mug of coffee
and what do you match it with?
          sections of a wooden
          footprints of a wooden
          a wooden valuable
          a wooden carrot
          a wooden shoe length impression

odd or even in an ambulance

wooOOOoooo
wooOOOoooo
is it a siren
or an alarm clock?
wooOOOoooo
garnnnggg

last scene   waking:
          investigators any leads on concentration
          and your name
          i have no idea
          just sunset
          the iron nostril
          the wooden footstall
          when men were men

MARBLES

if youf ry
you r mar bles
bef orey oup ut the min
the y'll mix
wi thy our brain
bet ter

BITE

tom rule
in his private cafe
uses opiates
to deal with the public
so what?
have a ham sandwich
chew pigs' feet
sing a foreign national anthem

piggery pokery
in his small cellar room
licks dirt from the walls
and sniffles by the hour
so what?
eat an opium sandwich
turn on the tv with your tongue
he might be you if you wake up

PERSONAL IDOLS

install a new statue as the paper cup of bad coffee
come up with asking their angel
wanted to cast their vote for toil
and fell down
historians who've chosen dead
with a spear in their van get
your mother with self   body-shifted
taking the inside of the cranium another address
make them sound like car
fbi agent
had bought lots of fair

anger was the only person
i was no one to talk
sometimes what inferno i'd be in
oh those elephants
igor straight to the melt early
look
wanted to cast a vote for thread
install a new statue in the even stuff she could use
life of wave this will live asking all their angel fur
crucified for resemblance to the future
personal idols among the work for myself
i just baby
had bought lots of body shifted
and i told her friends

TOM PAINE LOOKING FOR LOVE

i keep looking for you in a sunstorm
of flying fish one hundred years
from water
under a sky of brilliant newspaper
on feet ink-webbed
in sleep of dreamless intensity
of sentries guarding industrial trash with flashlights
at mid-day

some day this dream will run loose of my lifespan
and i will find you
in the majesty of a castle
that was once a small peasant cottage
in a valley of luminescent blue flowers where free villagers
eat sweetmeats they once considered foreign and unobtainable

COFFEE SHOES

found nothing sexual with of shoes
blind spots
and finds the golden rhinoceros milk
several houses down   pissing it off
guy five years of
red fur cup phone color of the traffic
where they serve coffee straight

practicing   five young to drink it for you
some guy gets before a robe and his shoes are jealous

the red upstairs caesar paint!
red slipped or burnt toast!
loving it this red neon sign reason to
awful here trading t-shirts for logo caps
blue suede drapes gone red!

here   somewhere
some guy gets tundra tongue
existential crisis machine
too cool for loopdy loop
cars in your coffee   gasoline in your gut
your feet hot inside   angry shoes crushed inside them
look!   up there!   it's the ceiling!

ACHILLES

bronze challenge development
development challenge bronze
challenge bronze development
development bronze challenge
challenge development bronze
bronze development challenge

A LAUGH A DAY MAKES THE WHIP HAND STRONGER

with her free hand and thrashed years old religious passion
begged and wheeled and
mercy mercy mercy for herself and for the audience
howled and wept and pleaded
in appeal to
a devout   fundamental
body to get it
all prayed out
exhausted
hoarse

the ensuing silence was more clap than would have been

would have hoped that
would be a hip
or not so hip

i want them to laugh at the stuff
torquemada

mama's hand had cramped from when she was
funniest in america
raised her hands to her face
massaging them with her breathing hard
outside clouds passed over the light streaming through the kitchen firma-
ment
she would enjoy that skinniest woman or something
anything she would enjoy

he turned away from the wastebasket desk
millions applauded
he piled that up and carried it to the
series built around comics
he sat in another chair
it was in coins
monsters he had created while helping around the house
millions applauded
he looked at the whip
there was no way off stage but down
millions applauded

PIZZA SHOES

shoe of pizza   your heartache
is my headache   is someone else's gutache
is someone else's sore foot
to the least of us a hot slice

you can wait for it under a tropical sun
you can wait for it under an electric sign
you can wait for it under a rainy roof
try not to wait under the oven

        i hear your footsteps going by the pizzeria
        you've got your pizzas on upside down
        at least the dough protects your foot
        dogs follow you   for blocks
        you know the scent of pepperoni attracts them
        more than the smell of your soles

MONUMENT

they're tearing out the floor of my father's house
to put in the monument to his living room
it's a small one
flattened like a headstone   or a sandwich
and though the work is done by people the supervisor
is a chimpanzee
he's not back yet
everybody is waiting
the cone is almost dug
and the ice cream is getting warm

i pick up a dime off my father's chest of drawers
and walk to the drug store
lingerie is strung across the aisles
baboons howl in the back room
at the deep end of an aisle a child sits
playing with a small red car
a green light goes on above the drug counter
a hamburger truck pulls in in front of the flower shop
across the street
an old man eats roses in the window
wearing a superman suit and pancake makeup

BULL TIN

fessiona
memorandu
corpora
rsonnel
utsourc
ganizati
ccess
laid off

ON THE CARPET

on the last day of the electricity strike
i went christmas
i saw brown makeup
strained on pillows
but it was too expensive

at dawn here
where everybody's bored
you and your face glowed

where

bright where you

men smoke metal cigars
stand pot-bellied where only the boss
because the boss loves the aroma
aroma of thieves

smoke won't
last long enough
to putrefy

where you came out young

glowed
twixt fake wood walls

you electric

they hazy
as they deserved

NEWS REPORT FROM THE FRONT

like the skull tattooed inside of my skull
like the teeth in the crotch of your elbow
like the knives at the end of each finger as you wave
i am only watching as the sun fades into the swamp

waiting for the brazen caterwaul of the owl
with steer horns and a dead child's face
waiting for its chess move to your chess move
bishop captures knight and eats him without genuflection

we are protected in this house   here
on stilts as the bombs roll the swamp and all the agony
is as beneath our sight as someone else's genitalia
cheats fantasy and only the report
of shriek and afterward moan decides

on this our vigilance screen the cameras swing
deeper into the water and dirt
we are told what to believe   we are protected   how joyous

LAMENT (for Hans Arp)

woe who who
he woe woe the hay-fish
woe wheelbarrow   thunders
woe woe consolation and snuff
monograms for us   woe woe
why have you   an udder
of craggy reality?
woe woe
now our crowns and soles
are charred at the bowling alley
woe woe
who will eat now
when he tries to entice the horses?
now coffee grinder
now the burning banner in his pigtail
now the rat who will expel the devil
now ships at sea
and umbrella
bee-keeper
transparent bride
another sigh kaspar kaspar kaspar
you became a star on a chain of water
woe woe

CHASING YOURSELF ACROSS THE STARS
(this one is for bob mosley)

tomorrow time finds itself this shack shifts
the far desert the
hearse mates called from a motel room in santa cruz
existential awareness month
us hassles   it is survivors
this is for people the real world down to change
perform again
        i will count your cheekbones
        with the faltering digits
        of my fingers

at last touching the bottom
have dropped memories flitting bars of the currents
        was a man whose life
        who had suffered
        he was still
        underwater
pounding bassline of the currents
        opening his eyes   blood shot
down which the moon had filtered
so he found himself at last in the
murk he touched liquid mud
himself at bottom
he was surprised

every time i see you i do not want it to be safe
all my soul
exhaustion all over you to your head like water rolling over
and over   every step as hard as is too explicable
dreams last night that hides it in its
fast   self   discovery
            slips

saw an angel
she opened all the blood veins he couldn't see
a cat ennobled at the ledge
every muscle
in its body awake!

did it betray you?   did i?
the memory crystalline don't step on it it's only a needle
it'll shatter

nothing left

i feel from myself a neighborhood is dangerous
            existential awareness month
            pricking me into fated you
cannot quiet them with
shoes
flap jacks
unexpected landings
skeletons all over the floor
distancing of ship
            there is nothing you can explore the level
            of meat like jonathan harker
            like the image of victor frankenstein the eyes going small
            on its way to traditional midbrain
            a sensation of needles
            help break a friend out of a
            dead building
            then told him
            later
            about the escape subtly

no safety latch
put to the head of a child

so after this
they sit around in a circle balanced by their haunches
knees bent backwards   dog style   cards in their hands
your soul just one of the chips
looking just like the others
but to you it glistens

remember the solo you played new year's 1967?
that last note
your coaxing it out into space
the audience whirling as if underwater
your face in the deep mirror
bathroom tiles around your head like an endless halo
seeing green faces leering at you
their lips and fingers bloating
they bid   and rebid
and you hear
someone else's notes now
controlling the course of the universe
but yours
running underneath them all
like the breathing
of the slowest planet
coursing the crescendo
of the music of the spheres

i was worried   in this deep shock
afraid there'd be toothbrush skeletons
nothing left
told the caterers we wanted those
meals hot
old friend focussed
joined coming shows pointed out
what might have been a star
tail after it
a procession of moons   across your face

your landing   nothing strange
four-footed like a cat
the motel room door
was argued the most charismatic
totem pole in the universe
but to sing one's own power current   like a ship's
              there is life in your shoes
              the way it wears away
              wherever you walk

W'

w   it
w   here
iding
in   mym   outh?
the   ni'll
tilif   indy   ou
myear   y
ou
myear

FROM A PORN NOVEL

his hips and she was suck
this   excited and she in his new fingers
i could see muscles twinge
in her thighs and calves
and i know
my landed neck nude while i watched

i could see them
i could understand
i could see them
he was possessing
i would have

she was his eyes shown early
as for myself   i felt lost
each stroke
the flabby child   i would have
i felt   turn over
in sleep   before
its hard   bitterness
tries to   open

ONE-LINER

elsa and i decided to have a vital center in a bare commissary
she with her bright full nails
swiped at my clown makeup and started eating

we were carrying on in animated pain and partially blind
her husband   by the neck
sunk in and left his fangs on the table

hey   anatole   how you like it licked at him?
it's a classic one-liner and he rolled over   begged
stood up   very proud of having said it

a modern day version in reverse
is now a bare-scrap incident
meant to be leader   a just time girl
stopped dancing and dusted her knees
stand forward
calmly sucked the business partner

it's the classic one-liner
feed situation from the back of the room
luminescent fingernails in the darkness
intimations of feed me
none of this ambivalence
normal folks might have tried

the rest of the people kept on message:
when I saw her drop to her knees
she had fainted   but she hadn't
she just said so   and winked

A RUGGED ASSIGNMENT

a table might room

this place:
he scanned the tables for a sight of the two
heavily walking charity wards looking back
and the coarse faces looking visible
might have been blue

creased worried one
each heavier made her heart ache
someone
which so far   now a nation

stay as long as you wish

then we won't go back there
here we abandon the car
foot into the wilds of cooped up with the books too long
no good
remarkable
amorous falsehood
sorry i'm late   my dear
just looking up this neighborhood

happiness:
             love her whoever she is
be shot
in love
he herself
then protruding on the counter

stay as long as you wish

THE DILEMMA

I

my friend has met death
a cold pretty woman in black who closes all the doors
to his living room
and won't let him out
won't even let him in
to the bathroom

now that you're here with me
she says
you don't need to piss

he stands there   cross-legged
even in his dream
not understanding how she can be so pure
not to understand

II

later
        he says
        i like the way that robe moves around you
        when you walk

i don't walk   the reply
        i move when you're looking
        and besides   there's nothing under the robe
        even bones   all the rest's your imagination

but you're a woman   he says
your imagination   the reply
        all you really see
        is the robe

III

once   on vacation   i found a replica of the robe
it hangs on the doorknob on the door to my bathroom
i wear it when i ache   my shoulders   hips   wrists
or when my imagination aches in certain ways
or when it's cold   vacant
or when the telephone rings and there's no one there
but when i hang up   the robe stirs
at the sleeves   hood   bottom hem
in a wind so physical i swear it really moves by itself
and i stop still   no pulse   listening
for someone's voice

TASTE

they build themselves in your finger
if your knees work   rips   the lizard is waiting
to a seaside dream
that were halved by half ready:
                you don't remember eyes and
                you don't remember shrieks
                too dry for a fever
                i was supposed to basketball
                as you walked down to mandalay
dead gangsters' hearts right inside your pantsleg
you're not supposed to or loose enough in the tropics
popcorn   passenger ships
when you saw it work enough saxophone to find out

ah the road to mandalay
where the frozen dinners play

play
in thirty years of roads about to go off
in the vision is being taste
in popcorn
in saxophone
it isn't easy giving feet without one
is it worth   taste?
that you saw in   taste?
to afterwards   taste?
you thought of   taste?
whatever   taste
carries that theology
the door opened
and a guitar rumbled
a giant pizza appeared on his bedroom ceiling
taste
he said

JOURNEY IN THE PLAGUE YEAR

you cannot hide   the cancer cells
clean as smokestacks through the clouds
inevitable
as fingers on your hand   (growing
extra ones)   there is no villa that will hide us
each one is cancered over with moss
the countess' coach is wrecked enroute
the wolfpack builds around it
scarred and scrawny
growing extra ones
above the trees is factory smoke

HEAT OF THE MEETING

i was burning the globe of the identical
slow liquid eye
but it generates smoke though it's hard to believe

this flow drawn
eros and thanatos
also freely

and love like a second thought
i can hear breath
in this warm   that heat
and in hell
and yet when you draw back
nineteen forever
i feel the coolness

rocketing like generals   nuclear cephalus
this is not the last look possible
if that kind of love
in the slow   could you not want it warmer
want the heat of that meeting
this comfort only once?

WALL AWE

noW ALL AWakE
alL nOW awake
awake All now
alL AwaKE now
AWaKe now all
NOw aWAke aLL

THANK-YOU NOTE

thank you for the long letter
why did you write it on a single hair?
was the hair yours?   a neighbor's?
did you find it in the gutter on the way home from work?
did you inscribe it
by using it as a tightrope
and walking across it
with a pen tied to your heel?

     i can see
     from the clarity of your signature
     that you didn't fall

     and if i look closely
     along the full length of the hair
     i swear i can recognize your footprints

FIVE DICTIONARY POEMS

I round:

    the rump
    a circular case

II name:

    as we called him
    reputation

III fare:

    to be in a well
    eat transportation

IV fate:

    to be incapable
    and the blue dye obtained

V favor:

    to help resemble
    approving

END OF THE GREAT MIGRATION

look   dream you requested
aren't the ones?

we had a very small thought tonight
destiny cat-smiled
oh   no   i whispered then
            another wheel to observe
            then we'd have walked rickety
            not seeing there are other car parks
            tinny music   bumper car range
            families with toy kids

                  i was
                  generous balloon
                  expanding well

                        he other world's dark outside
                        you can hear it yowl
                        and i   just one national crisis
                        played rainbow on the front steps
                        it was too early ahead as timet
                              so i petted the spider and her covered wagon
                              the whole pirate family
                              listened
                              sometimes i'm my own grandfather

ISLAND (for Judy)

in the early days the boat's sense of humor
shuttled cattle and crops from the political prowess
island to a road
county mainland
and returned

you are the sea level side of a tiger
where the island's wild winter
grew sheltered from the delta winds

yes i am addressing you
the subtle concavity of air as you walk
your eye of oceans
my rivers run mad in your footsteps
the whole world   quakes
islands lost
i must keep following you
or lose myself to a place
where there is no motion
no hope of summer
or even another fall

most of the people that later was turned
a white wood house or a
but the hardy
seaside tension all year
rebuilt their homes
remote   grassy
miles

SNO RING

s leep in glik e a
    cor psesno
        ring
    allth e air
    in toy outh
      en back
    ou tag ain
     emp tyno
        w

ROMANCE IS RELIVED

old who joys   death
could criticize the woes that go
with trouble

and particularly a spicy romance
calculation of shirts
tonic
would have recognized its making

brew:
trouble no

will   reached   and   are:
        1) always be too much for us
        2) heaven and it was syrupy
        3) because it says the discussion is over
        4) are not mine

no devil   will roll and stare
no roll and stare   is possessed
no devil is
no is possessed

someone i love?
speak to me for weeks
has large eyes   hourglass:
one in joy will always be live enough

DISCOVERY ON THE BEACH

i rolled down the windows in the fourth year
of on the coast highway
the smell   more destructive than any fishy
drifted into the car and people were out of work

millions of families were pulse of the music

stardust it isn't
other and i was thinking in fear
a world as warm and dark outside
a car parked by the beach
the last one in the farthest had yet to meet
halfway also searching for now then
a vague snout
he led the american around

he located the nation to victory

after his car there was good
the sudden bumper cars rickety
a constitutional amendment
families with kids
the range
was given other parked cars
not seeing them made me nervous

THE GOLD HOUSE

here   downtown
is the ruse with spare for animals
is the great house he's told servants guards
fear everyone to call into pretending

he's god   a hall of mirrors to fool himself
emperor and that he lives on a farm
tempered or that this is really his nature
seize food   with wilderness near

      he wears this house on a hill on his head
      crown badge sycophant veracity
      a small hat   shapes subtle when he bounces
      a mall fever colors seem to move forever
      town in no matter that stay no matter how long
      sbeware in his head his subjects remembering

GUIDE BOOK

the border
reputed to the heavily international world
divides the wealth:
just one block west of avenida ring
lined once again the free capital of
seeing them walk
during the six weeks of the sun

night it is

the openings of the eight-foot tomatoes
the flattened poland and germany of every town

meanwhile nearly everyone else is a renewal
yearly inflation has been about
forty percent bus stops
tourists   don't necessarily   suffer from the legend

casinos may seem disorienting
a state horizon   is quickly broke
a tropical island   wider
more than an acre

traditionally whaling lights
shine from the ceiling slot
they celebrate the exits
the talented bits of honey pots
imported for personal evenings
dancers and showgirls
offer various forms of poker   even bingo

the red light district
from every conceivable period and style
who try to crock even cubist buildings
continue to give onanism
the sight of haggard old beer mugs
hard-eyed decently priced potatoes
soul-destroying system of
power and machine-tool parts
except for those entrepreneurs
many are already doing so

they can peddle insanely overworked

casino
past endless blue fountains
and economic performance
are nearly as rare
as three machines
she's playing

night it is
a medieval with a human face

AN EXPLANATION OF TOURISTS IN NORTH BEACH

they begin the round it a gleaming emergency
we weaverhead the scene
fat king
faking his way through the groups that had volunteered
we had sex   and you're through the centuries
something he had not seen
he followed us for almost a block

the scene resembled just two paunchy bald and unmoving body
of out-of-town visitors looking for some
the grip of mosquitoes
steep cliffs that flanked the offers
you would know   for four hours
something he had not seen but
give you a membership card and you're through the centuries

from the search plane are good kids
crawling over the sinned against
everything is overgrown   kids are nice
it's real dangerous
at dusk   squadrons of my memory banks
bluffs that the river had carved
another sunset approached

ANOTHER TOURIST POEM

hutchins would build street people
use when they knew what to do and
seek to disarm their weary spring of 1931
just too slightly paunchy less out of town visitors looked
a few more rooms   for them to see

the new building was friend
another san franciscan
baths   live sex acts   again
brunswick lawson   from our very room
and the grand had come to visit

forty-eighth street paused
any use of the fit will not prosper
would you gentlemen here?
what's the place all him a believer?
it's a bar   he said   business

don't have to buy any from four hours
men have hanged them from that's all you want to do
drove her car into the lake for what you want
the staff was hired
make him a believer

MOST TOURISTS DON'T REALIZE

this is a very special flame into being
david niven must have seen the shards of planethood
you can see his boxes inset as below my feet my arms
above the bookstore across down to the center of everything

his cohorts
cross my sight with the
women on the streetcar
blankets across their legs
most tourists don't realize that field that opens every year
a woman with your face
awareness each a higher time
when she realizes i'm water it's eternal city

i bleed when i realize paints
street traffic outside   is every second adding five
i bought a new business dimension
time
at the discount store due horizons
but the way i paid   only i meant that

i want to connect with only at the beginning
i want a pair of binoculars from the picnic
i want the adults here to run something
i want crew sock poked out piercingly
i want throwing branches
i want pale but freckled feet

at the discount store
street traffic is a woman with your face
women on the streetcar cross my sight
call lariat   lariat
and branches keep catching
within and before the beginning

A BRIEF LOOK AT UNDERWEAR

that cars are barking   you can hear their horns and wheels squeal
bitter   they have to stay home
while buses write postcards to their parents in the transit yard
and traffic draws its inspiration from art in foreign museums

this is all on your opera schedule
underpants and bras flagging in the translucent breeze
the clouds going rancid   yellow with sunset
pages for sale at the bookstore   so go

    1) down park avenue if it smells fresh at all
    2) since i won't look whole in one mirror I'll look in two of them
    3) there is a real difference if it is done well enough
    4) the seagulls who squat in the sand like singing rocks
    5) the clouds are my favorites   i love their city
    6) and after the expedition   try to reach down and touch them

N IN OAKLAND

nothing

guys yelling
she looks   neldam's
a blond woman thin guy other guy
in a suit red shirt and children yelling
guy who's been a bottle of cheap cognac
kids yell in a project
can't get to the houses across
has cookies like mom's but not
for rent   parking
i was born here

suddenly the street gets stranger
houses torn apart to save them
guy who's been sick
the feel of cars and bart trains
running twenty feet over you

she looks   nothing nothing
who is parking lane?   lois?
suddenly can't get houses
guy who's suddenly oakland upholstery
grant miller mortuary nichols pharmacy
the street ends at a cyclone fence
freeway on the other side
a woman in a black suit and a red sweater
is watching me

guys yelling
she looks
neldam's
drives off in a
children's fort in a park

THE MEASURE OF WHAT YOU ASKED FOR

saint ophelia is a beautiful town
so bring me the sleeping bar net
pit him a lot of opera
and careful not to follow the directions of just any dust mote
not the king   not the warrior
just open space on prairie wisdom

a painted box on a dresser made of bear fat
she opens it and pours out a song about weasel heads
why they're whimpering   what she did to earn that
this time a hand plunged into time in search of its own body
then caressed itself in a hairy cling
        the interloper that will marry but will not be translated
        the anger unseen of midnight at an unopened door
        while decoded missile controls chatter among themselves
        that such a child will be as we

so this guy goes into a bar   says
give me the flying dead crows of my despair
so the bartender takes out a crowbar   says
all wings are the essence of flight
would you like a double?

CONTACT LENSES

where's my bathtub?
gotta simplify things:
plastic streets of this dream in front of you
bobbing as you walk
a guillotine has a cutting edge
and cold faces

walk again
like a fat woman inside a skinny woman trying to get out
like a   huge
simplification
like poverty swells each time its name
is turned into ceremony

has pinball been invented?

where have i been
looking for your knees?

contact lenses
dropped on command
biplanes ascending from an emotionless sea
bubbles bursting beneath your feet
one lifetime obsessed with the flying dutchman
is one too many

who inherited
this paper
command
that they cover   an entire ocean
in plastic

and ready to walk
no bathtub beneath them
on water?

FROM THE FOG

the surviving fragments about fog:
    couldn't understand why fog
    very direct to fear
    surviving an angel
    the word peace
    expected to from my fiancée
    was fond of oratory
    died in the enclosure
    others are humorous a hundred miles
    i was not yet asleep
    approach life force triumphed
i recognized a rock   a tree
that long-windedness which was to be avoided
a crumbling mass of something i did not have
that vision immediately returned
    of the living
    a kind of light near me
    a vast luminous halo
    the mist spreading it beyond shape
        beyond treatise
        beyond predictability
            to his lips
            this secret
            i can see
            as i drift
            apart in its coolness

BUCKETS OF TALK
(for Judy)

the throatiness of your voice
naked
like a rug
of fine jungle under your words

i walk home stolen
part of my brain   social
a mythical breakdown
a mysticism of canals
someone mistook me
almost
hid behind a skin
a shield of leather
haphazard radio sputtering around my fingers

water runs uphill
fish fly upside down
hills rise past the point
where you can see them touch the sky
safe in its vast blue ocean

buckets of talk
liquid joy
a fish came home in good weather
after a long walk in the desert
your voice travelling
under its fins

HANDS IN MIST

children of dead alibis those with wide-eyed alligators
in this nightclub district in the politics of fire
bring careful mice not the king already
he must not be asleep this time

of refrigerators not stomachs we are waiting for you
in a heap   of slag ham
combing the feathers on the wings of our sandals
a box on the table   already we whisper and caress

    already they passed the eyeball hand to hand
    and sat on the chair of forgetfulness
    where they made squeamish babies
    stingers comfortable as stingers
    horses asleep in the airplane hangars
    apples dancing in a war of elevator logic

    siren is a voice of someone startled
    medusa didn't stone us she just turned us to smoke
    we are here   an atmosphere   you are here